Share It!

Workbook

5

Cheryl Pelteret

macmillan
education

Table of Contents

1 Complete. Use the classroom rules below.

> ~~to your teacher~~   others   everything you need to class   the school rules
>   polite language   nice things to others

Be respectful!

Listen ___to your teacher___ .

Use _____ .

Please ... Thank you!

Be kind!

Help _____ .

Say _____ .

That's a great idea!

Be responsible!

Bring _____ .

Follow _____ .

I have my books!

2 What other classroom rules do you know? Write two more. Then draw.

_____   _____

3 Circle the correct numbers.

1 The Eiffel Tower is three hundred twenty-four meters tall.

(a) 324   b 3,024   c 30,204

2 Mr. Smith is one hundred one!

a 1,001   b 101   c 110

3 My dad has two thousand two hundred twelve pictures on his computer.

a 2,212   b 2,012   c 22,012

4 That rock is more than five million years old.

a 50,000,00   b 5,000   c 5,000,000

5 Nineteen thousand sixty people live in this town.

a 19,600   b 1,960   c 19,060

6 Twenty-four million six hundred thousand people live in Australia.

a 26,400,000   b 24,600,000   c 24,600

4 Complete. Use the words below.

> shorter   cm   kilometer   taller   centimeters   km

1 There are 100 _centimeters_ in a meter.

2 There are 1,000 meters in a _____.

3 We use _____ for kilometers.

4 We use _____ for centimeters.

5 141 centimeters is _____ than 140 centimeters.

6 143 centimeters is _____ than 144 centimeters.

Years

5 Write the dates. Choose from the dates below.

| 1996 | 1717 | 1800 | 1928 | 2010 | 1982 | 1777 | 2012 |

1 two thousand ten   _2010_

2 nineteen eighty-two   _____

3 seventeen seventy-seven   _____

4 two thousand twelve   _____

5 eighteen hundred   _____

6 nineteen ninety-six   _____

6 Read and write the numbers.

1
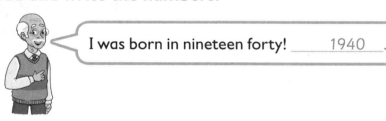
I was born in nineteen forty! _____1940_____.

2
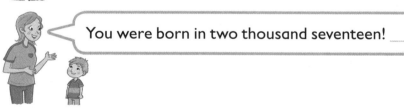
You were born in two thousand seventeen! _____

3
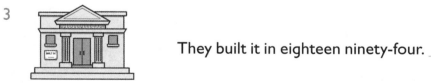
They built it in eighteen ninety-four. _____

4

His team won the match in two thousand sixteen. _____

5
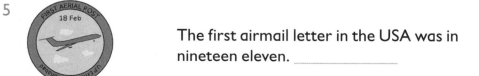
The first airmail letter in the USA was in nineteen eleven. _____

7 Read and complete. Use the words below.

| older | oldest | shorter | shortest | ~~taller~~ | tallest | younger | youngest |

My name's Amy! I was born in 2008.

I'm Rory. I was born in 2011.

I'm Alfie. I was born in 2014!

1 Rory is ___taller___ than his brother, Alfie. But Amy is the _____.
  She's 143 cm tall!

2 Alfie is the _____ and the _____.

3 Rory is three years _____ than Amy.

4 Amy is the _____. She's six years _____ than Alfie.

5 Rory is about 10 centimeters _____ than Amy.

8 Look again and write the names.

1 Who was born in two thousand fourteen? _____

2 Who was born in two thousand eleven? _____

3 Who was born in two thousand eight? _____

9 Answer the questions.

1 How old are you? _____

2 When were you born? _____

3 Are you the oldest/youngest in your family? _____

4 Who is older/younger than you? _____

5 Who is the tallest/shortest in your family? _____

6 How tall is he/she? _____

1 Adventure Camp

Lesson 1 Vocabulary

1 Complete. Then match the pictures to the words.

> build   cook   go ×4   ride   ~~sleep~~

 **1**

a   _sleep_   in a tent   6

b _____ canoeing

 **2**

c _____ on a zipline

 **3**

 **4**

d _____ horseback riding

e _____ on a campfire

 **5**

f _____ hiking

 **6**

g _____ a shelter

 **7**

h _____ mountain biking

 **8**

Student Book page 10

1 Complete. Use the simple past form of the verbs below.

| build | cook | ~~go~~ | not go | ride | not sleep | sleep |

Last week, Sara went to Adventure Camp. It was fun. She liked it a lot. She ¹ _____went_____

horseback riding, and she ² _____ on a zipline. She loved the zipline! One day,

she and her friends ³ _____ a shelter in a tree. At night, Sara ⁴ _____ on a

campfire. She ⁵ _____ in a bed. She ⁶ _____ in a tent! She went hiking, but

she ⁷ _____ canoeing or mountain biking. There was no time!

2 Look at Activity 1. Write the correct sentences.

1 Sara went to Adventure Camp last month.

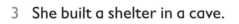

   Sara didn't go to Adventure Camp last month. She went last week.

2 She didn't like it.

   _____

3 She built a shelter in a cave.

   _____

4 She slept in a bed.

   _____

5 She went canoeing.

   _____

3 Complete. Use the simple past form of the verbs from Activities 1 and 2.

1 Last night, I (not) _____ in a tent. I _____ in my bed.

2 I (not) _____ on a campfire. I _____ in my kitchen.

3 I (not) _____ my bike. I _____ on a zipline.

4 I (not) _____ horseback riding. I _____ hiking.

Lesson 3 Reading

1 Read David's diary. Which activity did he like best? _____

It's Friday, and the end of my week at Summer Camp. Some things were good and some things were bad! We slept in tents. My tent was big. Four boys slept in it — Tom, Jack, Harry, and me. That was fun. On Monday, we went canoeing on the lake. I went in a canoe with Tom. We had a good time. And we cooked burgers on a campfire on Tuesday night. But the burgers were horrible! We had ice cream, too, and that was delicious. We rode on a long zipline on Wednesday! It was my favorite thing all week because it was scary, exciting, and fast! Yesterday, we went hiking in the mountains. But it was very hot and I was tired. Then we went swimming in the river. It was nice and cold! I loved it! Today was fun, too. We went mountain biking. I had a really good bike, so I was happy.

2 Read David's diary again. Then circle ☺ or ☹.

a my tent   ☺ ☹   b zipline   ☺ ☹

c canoeing   ☺ ☹   d hiking   ☺ ☹

e burgers   ☺ ☹   f swimming   ☺ ☹

g ice cream   ☺ ☹   h my mountain bike   ☺ ☹

3 Read David's diary again. Then complete.

1 David went to Summer Camp for a _____ week _____.

2 He slept in a _____ tent with _____ friends.

3 They cooked on a _____.

4 When he went hiking, the weather was _____.

5 It was nice to swim in the _____ river.

1 **Look at the Writing Tip. Write three more adjectives to describe places and activities.**

Places: big, _____cold_____, _____, _____

Activities: boring, fun, _____, _____, _____

> **Writing Tip!** Use adjectives to describe places and activities.
>
> *I went to Adventure Camp. It was **great**.*
>
> *I rode on a zipline. It was **fast** and **scary**.*

2 **Look at Activity 2 on page 13 of your Student Book. Write adjectives for the place you went to and the activity you did.**

Place: I went to _____.

It was _____ and _____.

Activity: I _____.

It was _____ and _____.

3 **Write your review. Use the information in Activity 2 of your Student Book and the adjectives in Activity 2 above.**

Name: _____

Title: _____

Date: _____

_____

_____

_____

_____

_____

☆ ☆ ☆ ☆ ☆

1 Complete the puzzle.

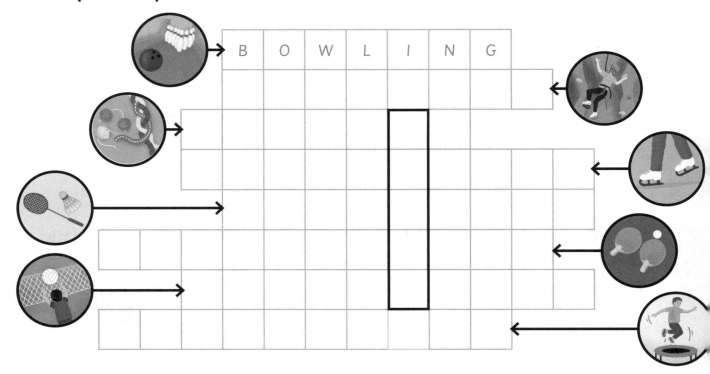

| B | O | W | L | I | N | G |

Write the hidden word. _____

2 Write the activities from Activity 1 next to the correct verbs.

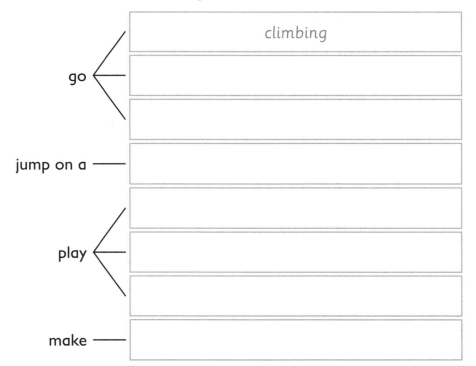

go — climbing

go —

go —

jump on a —

play —

play —

play —

make —

1 Complete the crossword. Use the simple past form.

Down	Across
1 jump	4 play
2 go	5 make
3 have	6 do

1 j
u
m
2
3   4 p
5   e
6 d

2 Read Kevin's answers. Complete the questions.

Grandma: Where ____did____ you _____ last week, Kevin?

Kevin: I went to camp!

Grandma: _____ you _____ a good time?

Kevin: Yes, I did. I had a great time!

Grandma: What games _____ you _____?

Kevin: We played volleyball and table tennis.

Grandma: _____ it rain?

Kevin: Yes, it rained one day, so we made jewelry. This necklace is for you!

Grandma: Oh, thank you! It's beautiful!

3 Write three questions to ask your friend.

1 What _____ yesterday?

2 Where _____ last week?

3 Did _____ yesterday?

Lesson 7 Social Studies CLIL

1 Circle the words. Then complete.

climbisledjewelefurjackhikintcompassbikskissheltracemountaiflag

1 Admundsen's team used dogs to pull their _____sled_____.

2 Explorers wore _____ jackets to keep warm.

3 The explorers used a _____ to find their way to the South Pole.

4 The explorers to the South Pole traveled on snow on _____.

5 Admundsen's team won the _____ to the South Pole.

6 Admundsen put Norway's _____ in the snow at the South Pole.

2 Match four words in Activity 1 to a–d in the picture. Write.

a _____

b _____

c _____

d _____

3 Read and match.

1 In 1911, two explorers, Scott, from England, and Admundsen, from Norway, …

2 Both teams slept in …

3 Scott and his team had a compass to find their way, but they didn't have …

4 Admundsen's team …

5 The team from Norway arrived …

6 The team from England …

a tents and wore skis on their feet to travel on the snow.

b never came home after the trip.

c started a race to the South Pole.

d first at the South Pole and put their flag in the snow.

e maps or fur jackets to keep warm.

f traveled fast, because they had dogs to pull their sleds.

1 Complete. Then match the pictures to the words.

a g____l

b t____tle

c h____t

d moth____

e sh____t

f wat____

1

2

3

4
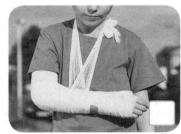

5

6

2 Complete. Then match the pictures to the sentences.

thirteen   surprise   teacher

a The bike is a great _____.

b My sister is _____ today.

c Do you like your _____?

1

2

3

Progress Tracker

1 Read and match.

1 You ride on …   a a trampoline.

2 You cook on …   b ice skating.

3 You play it with a ball.   c go climbing

4 We like to make …   d a compass

5 Last weekend, I went …   e a shelter

6 Dogs pulled …to the South Pole.   f jewelry.

7 Explorers used … to find their way.   g a zipline.

8 We built … outside and slept in it.   h a sled

9 You … in the mountains.   i a campfire.

10 You jump on …   j table tennis

2 Track it! Rate your progress in Unit 1.

I can name adventure camp activities.   ☆ ☆ ☆ ☆ ☆

I can make sentences in the simple past tense.   ☆ ☆ ☆ ☆ ☆

I can read and understand reviews.   ☆ ☆ ☆ ☆ ☆

I can write a review and give a rating.   ☆ ☆ ☆ ☆ ☆

I can name rainy day activities.   ☆ ☆ ☆ ☆ ☆

I can ask and answer questions in the simple past tense.   ☆ ☆ ☆ ☆ ☆

I can read and understand a true story about the past.   ☆ ☆ ☆ ☆ ☆

I can create and present information in a Venn diagram.   ☆ ☆ ☆ ☆ ☆

I can read and say words with -er-, -ir-, and -ur-.   ☆ ☆ ☆ ☆ ☆

Lesson 1 Vocabulary

1 Label the pictures. Use the words below.

1 _____sunbathe_____

2 _____

3 _____

4 _____

build a snowman
build a sandcastle
eat ice cream
go snorkeling
have a picnic
have a party
learn to ski
~~sunbathe~~

5 _____

6 _____

7 _____

8 _____

1 Read and complete. Use *was* or *were* (✔) or *wasn't* or *weren't* (✗).

What ____were____ you doing last weekend?

1 Alex, Spain

I ____was____ (✔) building a sandcastle on the beach. I was on vacation in Spain! The sun _____ (✔) shining, and it was hot. ☀

2 Olivia, England

It was my brother's 18th birthday. We _____ (✔) having a picnic in the yard! It's summer here, too, but the sun _____ (✗) shining. ☹ It was cloudy.

3 Ben, New Zealand

My sister and I _____ (✔) learning to ski. It's winter in New Zealand! That's why we _____ (✗) sunbathing on the beach. ⛷ ❄

2 Circle the correct form. Then answer the questions.

1 What (was) / were Alex doing on the beach?

   He was building a sandcastle.

2 What **was** / **were** the weather like in Spain last weekend?

   _____

3 Where **was** / **were** Olivia and her family having a picnic?

   _____

4 What **was** / **were** the children from New Zealand doing?

   _____

5 Why **wasn't** / **weren't** they sunbathing on the beach?

   _____

1 Read Dan's blog. Circle the best title for the blog.

  a The day I learnt to snorkel!   b Vacation memories   c Camping with my grandparents

2 Complete. Use the words below.

> ~~sunbathing~~   campfire   music   party   sandcastle   tent

My Holiday Pictures   By Dan

| HOME | ABOUT US | VACATIONS | FAVORITES |

 This was on our vacation last summer. We were at the beach. My mother was ¹ <u>sunbathing</u>, and my father was getting ready to go snorkeling. My sister and I were building a ² _____. My brother wasn't helping us. He was swimming in the sea.

 This is us in the mountains! We were camping. My father was cooking on a ³ _____, and we were helping him. We had a really nice day. But the next day wasn't great. It was raining, so we slept in our ⁴ _____ until lunch!

 In this picture, we were having a ⁵ _____ for my grandfather's birthday! It was nice and warm in the yard, and we were listening to ⁶ _____. The birthday cake was delicious! I am in the picture with my grandfather. Do you like our paper hats? I made them!

3 Read the blog again. Circle *True* or *False*. Then correct the false sentences.

1 Dan and his ~~brother~~ *sister* were building a sandcastle.   True / (False)

2 Dan's father was swimming.   True / False

3 Dan's father was cooking on a campfire at the beach.   True / False

4 The next day, at the campsite, it was raining.   True / False

5 Dan made paper hats for the birthday party.   True / False

Lesson 4 Writing

1 Look at the Writing Tip. Use commas to separate the items.

1 We were eating ice cream, cake and fruit.

2 I was listening to music sunbathing and having fun.

> **Writing Tip!** Use commas to separate three or more items in a list.
>
> *We were wearing shirts, jackets, and hats.*
>
> *I went canoeing, cooked on a campfire, and slept in a tent.*

2 Look at Activity 2 on page 23 of your Student Book. Write more words to add to your description of a vacation picture, so you can write lists and use commas.

_____

_____

3 Write your description of a vacation picture. Use the information in Activity 2 on page 23 of your Student Book and the words above. Remember to add commas to separate items in lists. Add your name and a title. Then draw your picture.

Title: _____ Name: _____

| HOME | ABOUT US | VACATIONS | FAVORITES |

1 Complete the crossword.

Across

1 sing in a …

3 do …

6 act in a …

7 tell …

Down

2 play the …

4 perform on …

5 watch the …

	¹B	A	N	²D			

2 Look and write the activities.

1

tell jokes

2

3

4

Lesson 6 Grammar

1 Look and complete the questions. Use *Was* or *Were*. Then write short answers.

1 <u>Were</u> two people singing?

   <u>Yes, they were.</u>

2 _____ a girl playing the drums?

   _____

3 _____ two children doing gymnastics?

   _____

4 _____ a boy telling a joke?

   _____

2 Cover the picture. What can you remember? Circle. Then write short answers.

1 (**Was**) / **Were** the cat sitting on the chair? <u>No, it wasn't.</u>

2 **Was** / **Were** the singers wearing hats? _____

3 **Was** / **Were** the teachers sitting down? _____

4 **Was** / **Were** the joke funny? _____

3 Circle. Then write three questions about the picture to ask a friend.

1 **Was** / **Were** _____ ?

2 **Was** / **Were** _____ ?

3 **Was** / **Were** _____ ?

1 Find and circle five words. Then complete the text.

f	o	r	g	e	t	b	t
t	i	p	s	o	b	r	e
x	p	x	t	c	a	a	s
a	d	d	a	v	v	i	t
p	p	h	s	z	l	n	k
q	z	s	g	m	k	o	c
r	e	m	e	m	b	e	r
j	o	u	r	n	a	l	h

Your body needs exercise. And your ¹ _____brain_____ needs exercise, too! What can you do to keep it heathy and strong? Here are some of our top ² _____!

Do puzzles, crosswords, and games — or try a spelling ³ _____. All these activities are good exercise for your brain!

Go to bed early! Try to sleep for eight hours a night, and then you won't ⁴ _____ important things the next day.

Write a ⁵ _____ every day. That way, you'll ⁶ _____ what happened. After all, memories are important.

2 Look at the words in Activity 1 and answer the questions.

1 Which two words are opposites? _____, _____

2 Which word means a "diary"? _____

3 Which word is a kind of quiz? _____

4 Which word is a part of the body? _____

5 Which word means "useful things to do"? _____

1 **Look and write. Use the words below.**

| car | star | shark | ~~farm~~ | jar | arm |

1 _____farm_____

2 _____

3 _____

4 _____

5 _____

6 _____

2 **Match the words to the pictures. Then complete the sentences.**

| barn | ~~dark~~ | large |

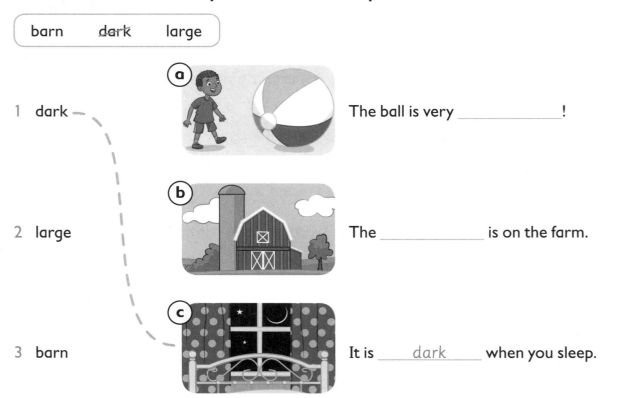

1 dark

a — The ball is very _____!

2 large

b — The _____ is on the farm.

3 barn

c — It is _____dark_____ when you sleep.

1 Match the words to the definitions.

1 It's something you do in the ocean. _c_

2 You can do this on the grass or at a table in the park. _____

3 It's fun to do when it snows, and dress it up in old clothes! _____

4 It's something you do in a play. _____

5 Some people do this for their birthday. _____

6 It's something you do at the beach. _____

7 When you do this, it makes people laugh. _____

8 It's something you do for good health. _____

9 It's a sport you can try in the snow. _____

10 It's something you do when it's sunny. _____

a build a snowman

b do gymnastics

c go snorkeling

d have a party

e have a picnic

f learn to ski

g perform on stage

h build a sandcastle

i sunbathe

j tell a joke

2 Track it! Rate your progress in Unit 2.

I can name activity verbs.

I can talk about what people were doing in the past.

I can read and understand descriptions of pictures.

I can write a description of a picture.

I can name entertainment activities.

I can ask what people were doing in the past.

I can read and understand a text about memory.

I can talk about ways to help my memory.

I can read and say words with -ar-.

Share the World 1 | Sally Ann Thunder Ann Whirlwind – A Tall Tale

1 Circle the correct answer. A "tall tale" is ...

1 always true.   2 not true.   3 sometimes true.

2 Circle the correct answers.

1 Sally Ann Thunder Ann Whirlwind was **tall** / **small** and strong.

2 She **could** / **couldn't** run a long way.

3 She saw 50 **snakes** / **alligators** coming to the house.

4 When she was 18, she went hiking **with** / **without** her family.

5 She **was** / **wasn't** scared when she met a **panther** / **bear** in a cave.

6 Davy Crockett **was** / **wasn't** happy to see Sally at the bottom of the tree.

3 Answer the questions.

1 How do you know Sally Ann was very good at swimming?

_____

2 What did she do when she saw the alligators?

_____

3 Where did she sleep when she went hiking?

_____

4 How did she cook?

_____

5 How did she run away from the bear?

_____

6 How did she help Davy Crockett climb down the tree?

_____

7 Who did she dance with on the way home?

_____

4 Look at your answers from Activity 3. Which sentences tell you that it is a "tall tale"?

_____

_____

5 Look at the pictures. Use different colors to make "tall tale" sentences.

1 Sally Ann ran faster	with a cute rabbit	in the forest.
2 Sally Ann ate dinner	with a happy raccoon	with a koala on her back.
3 Sally Ann danced	than a puma	in a cave.
4 Sally Ann climbed	the tallest mountain	in a field.

6 Write a "tall tale" sentence. Then draw.

_____

Lesson 1 Vocabulary

1 Complete the crossword. Then number the pictures.

Across

1 Every weekend, I walk the …

4 How often do you read the …?

6 It's my brother's job to take out the …

7 My dad is teaching me to play …

8 Tonight, I'm going to study for a …

Down

2 We buy … at the supermarket.

3 When it's my mom's birthday, I buy a … for her.

5 Every night, we watch the …

Crossword: 1 Across: D O G

a
4

b

c

d

e

f

g

h

Student Book page 34

1 Circle the correct form of the verbs.

1 They **watched** / (were watching) TV when the phone
was ringing / (rang).

2 I **took** / **was taking** out the trash when they **arrived** / **were arriving**.

3 When I **saw** / **was seeing** you in the store, you **bought** / **were buying** a present.

4 Tom and his mom **played** / **were playing** chess when they **heard** / **were hearing**
the news on TV.

5 We **walked** / **were walking** the dog when I **lost** / **was losing** my money.

2 Look and write. Use the correct form of the verbs.

1

They _were having_ (have) a picnic
when it _____ (start) to rain.

2

We _____ (build) a sandcastle
when we _____ (find) the old coin.

3

When I _____ (hurt) my leg,
I _____ (play) football.

4

Suzy _____ (eat) a sandwich
when a bird _____ (take) it.

Lesson 3 Reading

1 Read and check (✔) the correct picture for the news story.

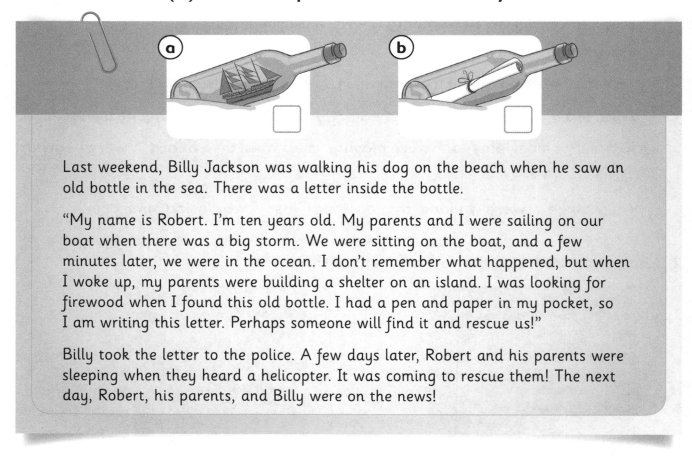

Last weekend, Billy Jackson was walking his dog on the beach when he saw an old bottle in the sea. There was a letter inside the bottle.

"My name is Robert. I'm ten years old. My parents and I were sailing on our boat when there was a big storm. We were sitting on the boat, and a few minutes later, we were in the ocean. I don't remember what happened, but when I woke up, my parents were building a shelter on an island. I was looking for firewood when I found this old bottle. I had a pen and paper in my pocket, so I am writing this letter. Perhaps someone will find it and rescue us!"

Billy took the letter to the police. A few days later, Robert and his parents were sleeping when they heard a helicopter. It was coming to rescue them! The next day, Robert, his parents, and Billy were on the news!

2 Read and match.

☐	a While they were on the boat	was lying on the sand.
1	b Billy Jackson	there was a storm.
☐	c Robert wrote	a helicopter came to rescue them.
4	d Robert and his parents	a letter and put it in the bottle.
☐	e They woke up	were sailing on a boat.
☐	f A bottle	was walking his dog on the beach.
☐	g While they were sleeping,	inside the bottle.
☐	h A letter was	on an island.

3 Number the sentences (a–h) in Activity 2 in the correct order.

1 Look at the Writing Tip. Use the words to order the events in the story.

First,   Finally,   Next,   Then,

1 _____ the monkey ran across the road. 2 _____Then,_____ it jumped up into a

tree. 3 _____ it threw a coconut at someone in the street! 4 _____ the

zoo rescued the monkey and took it back to its cage.

Writing Tip! Use *First, Then, Next,* and *Finally* to order events in a story. Add a comma after these words.

First, *we bought an ice cream.* **Then,** *we went to see the monkeys.*
Next, *we watched the elephants.* **Finally,** *we went home.*

2 Look at Activity 1 on page 37 of your Student Book. Then complete.

First, _____. Then, _____.

Next, _____. Finally, _____.

3 Write your news story. Use the information in Activity 2 on page 37 of your Student Book and the words above to order the events. Add a title for your news story.

_____

_____

_____

_____

_____

_____

Lesson 5 Vocabulary

1 Match the parts of the phrases.

1 go   a the radio

2 download an   b online

3 listen to   c at a screen

4 look   d posts

5 read   e app

6 read blog   f magazines

2 Complete. Use the words below.

> blog   download   online   listen   ~~look at~~   read   screen

I ¹ look at a screen every day. I often read ² _____ posts on my laptop. I also go ³ _____ to play games and to look up information for projects.

There are a lot of different ways to read the news on the internet! You can ⁴ _____ apps, for example. That's what I do!

I never read newspapers, but I often ⁵ _____ magazines. I also ⁶ _____ to the radio to hear the news. I don't think it's good for your eyes to look at a ⁷ _____ all the time!

1 Look and write the questions. Then answer them. Use the correct form of the verb.

1 What / you and your friend (do) when the bus (arrive)?

What were you and your friend doing when the bus arrived?

We _____were listening_____ (listen) to music when the bus

_____arrived_____ (arrive).

2 What / the waiter (carry) when he (stand) on a banana skin?

_____

He _____ (carry) a plate when

he _____ (stand) on a banana skin.

3 What / your mom (do) when she (hear) the news?

_____

She _____ (wash) the dishes when

she _____ (hear) the news.

4 What / you (do) when I (call) you?

_____

I _____ (sleep) when

you _____ (call) me!

5 What / they (look) at when the teacher (come) in?

_____

They _____ (look) at their phones when

the teacher _____ (come) in.

6 Where / the man (walk) when his hat (fall) off?

_____

He _____ (walk) in the park when

his hat _____ (fall) off.

Lesson 7 Social Studies CLIL

1 Circle the words. Then complete.

socialmedia(towncrier)becausemanypeoplestownsquarecouldn'tbellreadworldorlandedwrite

Long ago, people didn't have 1＿＿＿＿＿ ＿＿＿＿＿ to get the news! They

got the news in other ways. In the 17th century, they heard the news from a person

called the 2 _town crier_ . This person stood in the middle of the town, usually in the

3＿＿＿＿＿ ＿＿＿＿＿ . When he rang a 4＿＿＿＿＿ , people came to listen

to him shout the news!

Then, more and more people around the 5＿＿＿＿＿ learned to read. They started to

listen to the news on the radio and read newspapers.

Today, we sometimes hear the news before we see it on TV. For example, when an

airplane 6＿＿＿＿＿ on the Hudson River in New York, people learned about it on the

internet first.

2 Use the extra words in the wordsnake to answer the question: Why didn't people in the 17th century read newspapers?

＿＿＿＿＿＿＿＿＿＿＿＿＿＿＿＿

3 Label the picture. Use three words from Activity 1.

1 Who is he?

＿＿＿＿＿＿＿＿

2 Where is he?

＿＿＿＿＿＿＿＿

3 What is in his right hand?

＿＿＿＿＿＿＿＿

1 Match the pictures to the words.

1

2

a   corn

b   horse

3

4

c   fork

d   storm

5

6

e   snore

f   score

2 Look and complete. Use the words below.

wore   thorn   store

1

2

3

The flower has a
big _____.

The _____ sells
a lot of bikes!

She _____ a
beautiful dress.

Progress Tracker

1 Complete. Use the words below.

test   apps   ~~blog posts~~   chess   groceries   news
present   radio   screen   trash

1 You read newspapers and __blog posts__ .

2 You buy _____ to eat.

3 You play _____ .

4 You look at a _____ when you watch a movie.

5 You listen to music on the _____ .

6 You study for a _____ .

7 You take out the _____ .

8 You watch the _____ online or on TV.

9 You buy a _____ when it's somebody's birthday.

10 You can download _____ to play games on your phone.

2 Track it! Rate your progress in Unit 3.

I can name eight everyday activities. ☆☆☆☆☆

I can talk about what happened in the past with *when*. ☆☆☆☆☆

I can read and understand a news story. ☆☆☆☆☆

I can write a news story. ☆☆☆☆☆

I can name communication activities. ☆☆☆☆☆

I can ask questions about the past using *when*. ☆☆☆☆☆

I can read and understand a text about the history of news. ☆☆☆☆☆

I can make a time line and talk about the past. ☆☆☆☆☆

I can read and say words with *-or-* and *-ore*. ☆☆☆☆☆

Lesson 1 Vocabulary

1 Complete. Use *feel* or *have* and the words below.

| a cold | a fever | good | a headache | sick | a stomach ache |
| | | | a sore throat | | a toothache |

1 I _have a fever_ .

2 I _____ .

3 I _____ .

4 I _____ .

5 I _____ .

6 I _____ .

7 I _____ .

8 I _____ .

Lesson 2 Grammar

1 Match the questions to the answers.

1 Do you feel sick, Maya?

2 What's the matter?

3 Does Pablo have a fever?

4 Is Eddie OK?

a I have a toothache.

b No, he doesn't.

c Yes, I do.

d No, he isn't. He has a headache.

2 Complete. Use the correct form of *do*, *have*, and *feel*.

A: Does Jake 1 _____have_____ a stomach ache?

B: Yes, he 2 _____. He was eating sweets all day. Now he 3 _____ feel good.

A: What's the matter with Paulo? 4 _____ he feel OK?

B: No, he 5 _____. He 6 _____ a cold.

A: What's wrong with Janelle?

B: She 7 _____ a fever.

A: 8 _____ she have a headache?

B: Yes, she 9 _____. And she 10 _____ sick.

A: How do *you* feel?

B: I 11 _____ good, thanks!

1 Number the messages in the correct order (1–10). What's the matter with Amelia?

Amelia: No, I'm not. 😞 ☐

7 **Todd:** Poor you! Do you want me to bring your homework?

Amelia: Yes, I do. I have a headache and I feel sick, too. ☐

3 **Todd:** Why? What's the matter?

Todd: OK. Get some sleep. Feel better! 💪 ☐

1 **Todd:** Hey, Amelia! Why weren't you in school today? Are you OK?

Amelia: No, it's OK. I don't think I can study today. I feel very tired. ☐

Todd: A fever? Oh, no. Do you still feel bad? ☐

Amelia: I have a fever. ☐

Amelia: Thanks, Todd. ☐

2 Read and check (✔) or cross (✗).

1 Todd wasn't in school today. ☐

2 Amelia has a stomach ache. ☐

3 Amelia feels sick, has a headache, and has a fever. ☐

4 Amelia doesn't want to study today. ☐

Lesson 4 Writing

1 **Look at the Writing Tip. Write six capital letters in the formal email.**

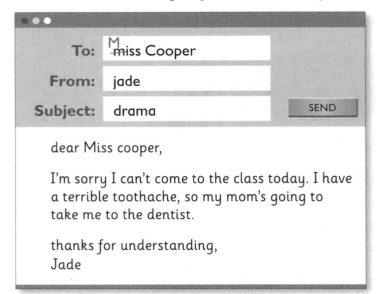

To: Miss Cooper

From: jade

Subject: drama

SEND

dear Miss cooper,

I'm sorry I can't come to the class today. I have a terrible toothache, so my mom's going to take me to the dentist.

thanks for understanding,
Jade

> **Writing Tip!** Use capital letters:
> * for titles and names of people.
> * at the beginning of a sentence.
> * in the subject line of an email.
>
> *My teacher's name is **M**iss **J**enny **M**oreton.*
>
> ***G**ood morning, **M**r. and **M**rs. **J**ones! **T**hanks for coming to our school.*
>
> ***S**ubject: **M**usic **P**ractice*

2 **Write your formal email. Use the information in Activity 2 on page 47 of your Student Book and the information above. Use capital letters.**

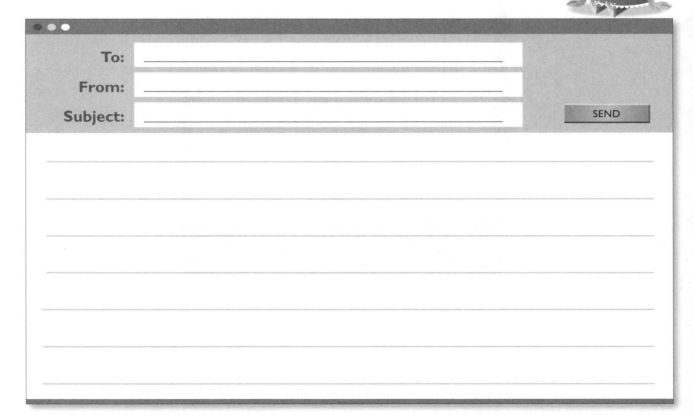

To: _____

From: _____

Subject: _____

SEND

_____

_____

_____

_____

_____

_____

1 Complete. Use the words below.

| cough | flu | lie down | medicine | pharmacy | symptoms | temperature |

Mom: What's the matter, Libby? You don't look well.

Libby: I feel terrible, Mom! I have a bad headache.

Mom: Oh, dear. Perhaps you have a cold. Do you have a sore throat and a ¹ _____cough_____, too?

Libby: No, I don't.

Mom: Do you have a fever?

Libby: I don't know. I feel very hot …

Mom: Let me see. Oh, dear. You have a high ² _____.

Libby: My body aches, too.

Mom: I think you have the ³ _____. You have all the ⁴ _____ of it.

Libby: Can I go to school today?

Mom: I'm sorry, but you can't. You have to stay in bed. Just ⁵ _____ and get some rest. When Dad comes home, he'll go to the ⁶ _____ and get some ⁷ _____ for you.

2 Answer the questions. Use the words from Activity 1.

1 Which one is a symptom of a cold?

_____

2 Which one is a store?

_____

3 Which activity can help you feel better?

_____

4 Which one can you buy to help you feel better?

_____

1 Write the questions. Use *should*. Then write answers.

1 I have a headache. What / I / do?

What should I do?

You should take some medicine.

2 Bobby doesn't feel good. he / go to school?

_____

_____

3 I feel sick. I / lie down?

_____

_____

4 Jonah has a stomach ache. What / he / do?

_____

_____

2 Read and check (✔) or cross (✗). Then write sentences for the advice.

"How to be healthy!"
"Is it a good idea to ...?"

• drink too much cola	✗	1	_You shouldn't drink too much cola._
• eat too much candy	☐	2	_____
• go to bed late	☐	3	_____
• eat fruits and vegetables every day	☐	4	_____
• play sports	☐	5	_____

Student Book page 49

1 Unscramble the words.

Be clean and stay healthy!

Do you have a cold?

Remember, [1] (mergs) _____germs_____ can travel a long way and very fast!

When you cough or [2] (enezes) _____, always [3] (verco) _____ your nose and mouth with a [4] (estisu) _____.

And always wash your hands with [5] (posa) _____ and water. That is the best way to [6] (lilk) _____ the germs that make us sick.

2 Read and match.

1 Germs give us   a   soap and water.

2 We use a tissue to cover our   b   germs.

3 When we sneeze, germs can travel   c   colds and sore throats.

4 We leave germs   d   a long way quickly.

5 Wash your hands with   e   on everything we touch.

6 Soap and water kill   f   mouths and noses.

3 How do you stay clean and healthy?

_____

_____

_____

Lesson 8 Word Study -ou-, -ow-

1 Look and complete the words. Use -ou- or -ow-.

1

m _o_ _u_ th

2

br _____ _____n hair

3

h_____ _____se

4

c _____ _____

5

d_____ _____n

6

m_____ _____se

2 Look and complete. Use the words below.

owl   found   crown   bounces

1

The queen has a big _____.

2
He _____ the ball.

3

The _____ sits in the tree.

4

She _____ a book in the park.

Student Book page 52

1 Match the words to the definitions.

1 These are two symptoms of a cold. _a_ , _____

2 You can buy this to help you feel better when you have a cold or feel sick. _____

3 You should cover your mouth with this when you have a cold or flu. _____

4 These are two symptoms of the flu. They make your head feel hot. _____ , _____

5 Go to this place if you aren't feeling good. _____

6 This kind of pain is in your mouth. _____

7 You should do this if you have a headache or feel sick. _____

8 This is similar to a cold, but you feel worse. _____

a a cough

b a fever

c flu

d a high temperature

e lie down

f medicine

g the pharmacy

h a sore throat

i a tissue

j a toothache

2 Track it! Rate your progress in Unit 4.

I can name health conditions. ☆☆☆☆☆

I can talk about illnesses. ☆☆☆☆☆

I can read and understand informal text messages. ☆☆☆☆☆

I can write a formal email. ☆☆☆☆☆

I can name words about colds and the flu. ☆☆☆☆☆

I can talk about health problems and give advice. ☆☆☆☆☆

I can read and understand a text about healthy habits. ☆☆☆☆☆

I can make a poster and talk about healthy habits. ☆☆☆☆☆

I can read and say words with -ou- and -ow-. ☆☆☆☆☆

Share the World 2 | Hygge

1 Circle the best example of a *hygge* activity.

1 Playing games on your tablet with your friends.

2 Sitting by the fire with your family and friends.

3 Watching and discussing the news on TV with your family.

2 Write the words and phrases under the correct headings. Then check (✔) the *hygge* activities.

> apple pie   warm socks   favorite sweater   hot chocolate
> play board games   watch the news on TV   listen to music
> look at your phone   watch a movie on TV   sit in front of a fire

Activities

1 play board games ✓   2 _____   3 _____

4 _____   5 _____   6 _____

Food   **Clothes**

7 _____   9 _____

8 _____   10 _____

3 Answer the questions.

1 Why do people often feel sick or sad in winter?

_____

2 Where does the tradition of *hygge* come from?

_____

3 When do people do it?

_____

4 Is it something we can all do? Why?

_____

4 Look at the chart. Write sentences with *hygge* advice. Use a word or phrase from each column.

You should	send	text messages.
You shouldn't	chat with friends and family	warm, comfortable clothes.
You should	watch	in front of a fire.
You shouldn't	wear	the news on TV.

1   You should chat with friends and family in front of a fire.

2   _____

3   _____

4   _____

5 Think about a *hygge* time in your life and answer the questions.

1   What were you doing?

   _____

2   Who were you with?

   _____

3   Where were you?

   _____

4   What was the weather like?

   _____

5   Why do you have happy memories of this time?

   _____

6 Why do you think people enjoy doing *hygge* activities?

   _____

   _____

5 Cook Well, Eat Well!

Lesson 1 Vocabulary

1 Complete the labels.

1 honey
2 s _ _ _ _ r
3 m _ _ _ r _ _ _ s
4 o _ _ v _ s
5 b _ _ t _ r
6 f _ _ u _
7 s _ _ _ wb _ _ r _ _ s
8 s _ _ t   p _ _ p _ r
9 j _ _ l _

2 Complete. Use the words in Activity 1.

1 I like bread with b _utter_ , j _____ , or h _____ on it.

2 Would you like some s _____ and p _____ on your French fries?

3 This ice cream is pink because there are a lot of s_____ in it!

4 My favorite pizza has cheese, m _____ , and o _____ on it.

5 To make pancakes, you need f _____ , b _____ , s _____ , and milk.

1 **Write six different sentences. Use a word or phrase from each column.**

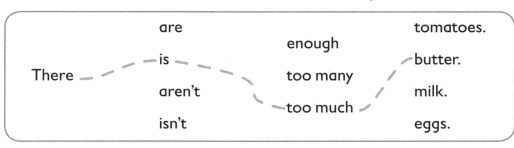

1 _There is too much butter._   2 _____

3 _____   4 _____

5 _____   6 _____

2 **Look and complete.**

1 Oh, no! There ____is too much____ jelly.

2 There _____ mushrooms on this pizza!

3 Sorry. There _____ olives. There's only one!

4 Stop! There _____ salt!

5 There _____ strawberries.

6 There _____ honey!

Lesson 3 Reading

1 Read. Then match the pictures to the days.

FOOD DIARY BLOG

DIARY I GALLERY I RECIPES

Thursday, March 11 ☐

Today, I had a healthy day. For breakfast, I had yogurt. For lunch, I didn't know what to have — fish and salad or chicken and vegetables. I had fish and salad — it was delicious! I had a banana and an apple as a snack. For dinner, I had chicken and rice. After dinner, we had some strawberries.

Friday, March 12 ☐

I had eggs for breakfast today, because I wanted to have a lot of energy for my soccer match after school. During the match, we had some oranges. We won the match! Our teacher bought us a big pizza! It was nice, but there were too many mushrooms on it (I don't really like them).

Saturday, March 13 ☐

It was Rory's birthday party. His mom made a strawberry cake. It had a lot of fruit in it, so it wasn't too unhealthy! But I had a lot of ice cream, too. I think I ate too much food, because when I got home, I had a stomach ache. I didn't want any dinner, so I just had some bread before bed!

1

2

3

2 Read the food diary in Activity 1 again. Then complete the chart.

	Snacks Between Meals	Healthy Meals	Too Much Sugar
Thursday	banana apple		
Friday			
Saturday			

1 **Look at the Writing Tip. Circle the correct words to link ideas in the sentences.**

1 The pizza was good, (**but**) / **and** it had too much salt on it.

2 I had yogurt for breakfast **or** / **and** a cheese sandwich for lunch.

3 Would you like some fruit before lunch **so** / **or** after lunch?

4 I wasn't hungry, **but** / **so** I didn't have any dinner.

Writing Tip! Use *and*, *but*, *or*, and *so* to link two ideas in a sentence to be on a new line. Use:

- *and* to add another similar idea. *Yesterday, I ate a lot of fruits **and** vegetables.*

- *but* to link two different ideas. *I like French fries, **but** they aren't very healthy.*

- *or* when there is a choice between different ideas. *For breakfast, I usually have cereal with milk **or** yogurt.*

- *so* to explain or give a reason for something. *I played football today, **so** I feel very healthy.*

---

2 **Look at Activity 2 on page 61 of your Student Book. Answer the questions.**

1 What food did you have? Was it healthy or unhealthy?

_____

2 Did you have too much or not enough of anything?

_____

3 **Write your food diary. Use the information in Activity 2 on page 61 of your Student Book and the information above. Use words to link ideas in the sentences.**

FOOD DIARY

Lesson 5 Vocabulary

1 Complete the puzzle. Then write the hidden word.

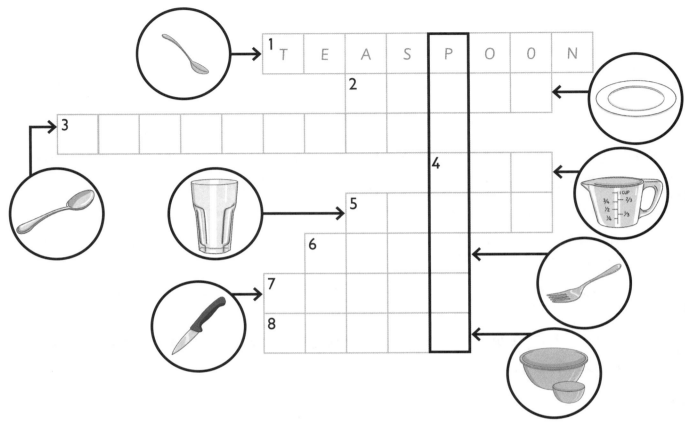

1 T E A S P O O N

Write the hidden word. _____

2 Answer the questions. Use the words from Activity 1.

1 What do you use to eat cereal or soup in? _____

2 What do you eat your dinner on? _____

3 What do you use to eat soup? _____

4 What do you use to cut fruit and vegetables? _____

5 What do you use to eat pasta with? _____

6 What do you use to drink milk or water from? _____

7 What do you drink coffee from? _____

8 What do you use to add sugar to a cup of coffee? _____

1 **Read the recipe. Complete the questions with _much_ or _many_. Then circle the correct answers.**

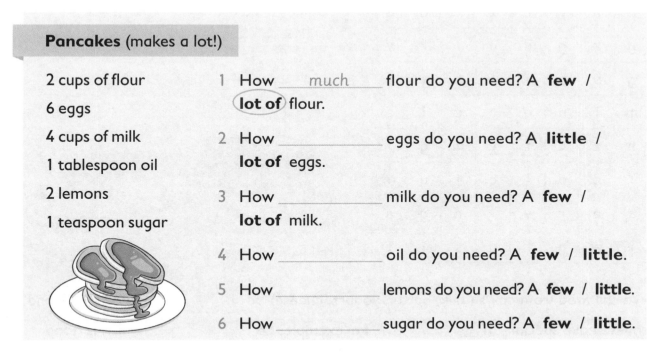

Pancakes (makes a lot!)

2 cups of flour

6 eggs

4 cups of milk

1 tablespoon oil

2 lemons

1 teaspoon sugar

1 How ____much____ flour do you need? A **few** / (**lot of**) flour.

2 How _____ eggs do you need? A **little** / **lot of** eggs.

3 How _____ milk do you need? A **few** / **lot of** milk.

4 How _____ oil do you need? A **few** / **little**.

5 How _____ lemons do you need? A **few** / **little**.

6 How _____ sugar do you need? A **few** / **little**.

2 **Look at the picture. Complete the questions and answers. Use _How much_, _How many_, _are there_, _is there_, _is/are_, _a lot of_, _a few_, or _a little_.**

1 ___How many___ carrots ___are there___ ? There ___are a lot of___ carrots.

2 _____ apples _____ ? There _____ apples.

3 _____ eggs _____ ? There _____ eggs.

4 _____ milk _____ ? There _____ milk.

5 _____ flour _____ ? There _____ flour.

6 _____ butter _____ ? There _____ butter.

Lesson 7 Science

1 Circle the words. Then complete.

p	n	y	r	z	v	o	q
g	z	g	d	a	i	r	y
w	p	b	i	w	t	t	p
m	i	n	e	r	a	l	s
h	z	c	t	y	m	g	f
f	c	a	l	c	i	u	m
s	e	r	v	i	n	g	s
j	w	n	h	q	s	i	t

We call food from cows (milk, butter, yogurt, cheese) [1] d _airy_ foods. Milk and cheese have special [2] m _____, for example, [3] c _____, which is good for our bones. We should have five [4] s _____ of fruits and vegetables a day. Our [5] d _____ should have all 13 different [6] v _____, for example, C (for healthy bones and teeth), A (for healthy eyes), and D (for strong muscles).

2 Look at the circled words in Activity 1. Answer the questions.

1 What word is the food you eat every day? _____ _diet_ _____

2 What word is how many bowls of food you have for breakfast? _____

3 What word is a mineral that is good for strong bones and teeth? _____

4 What word has, for example, C, A, and D? _____

1 Complete the sentences. Use the words below.

| pointing | toy | noise | coin | boy | boiling |

1

It's a ___coin___ .

2

The water is _____ .

3

The _____ is happy.

4

The girl is _____ .

5

There's a lot of _____ !

6

It's a funny _____ !

2 Complete the sentences. Use -oi- or -oy.

1

The boys are full of
j____ !

2

The flowers are
m____ st.

3

Amy and May j____ n
hands.

Progress Tracker

1 Label the food items. Use the words below.

bowl   fork   knife   mushrooms   pepper   ~~plate~~   salt   strawberries
sugar   teaspoon

For lunch, I had a ¹ _plate_ of ² _____. I put some

³ _____ and ⁴ _____ on them, and I ate them with a

⁵ _____ and a ⁶ _____. After that, I had a

⁷ _____ of ⁸ _____, with a ⁹ _____ of

¹⁰ _____ on the top. Mmm! Delicious!

2 Track it! Rate your progress in Unit 5.

I can name food words.   ☆ ☆ ☆ ☆ ☆

I can talk about quantities of food.   ☆ ☆ ☆ ☆ ☆

I can read and understand a food diary.   ☆ ☆ ☆ ☆ ☆

I can write a food diary and talk about the food I ate.   ☆ ☆ ☆ ☆ ☆

I can name items to use in the kitchen.   ☆ ☆ ☆ ☆ ☆

I can ask about food for a recipe.   ☆ ☆ ☆ ☆ ☆

I can read and understand a text about vitamins and minerals. ☆ ☆ ☆ ☆ ☆

I can talk about vitamins in food.   ☆ ☆ ☆ ☆ ☆

I can read and say words with -oi- and -oy.   ☆ ☆ ☆ ☆ ☆

Student Book page 67

Lesson 1 Vocabulary

1 **Complete the crossword.**

Across

3 We live on the ... Earth.

5 A ... is a big ball of rock, ice, and dust that travels through space.

7 A ... is a small object that we send into space from Earth to find information.

8 We can see the ... in the sky at night.

Down

1 A ... helps you to see faraway objects more clearly.

2 A ... takes astronauts into space.

4 Astronauts live and work at the space ...

6 Everything in our ... system goes around the sun.

```
                                  ¹T
                              ²   E
                                  L
                          3       E
                                  S
                  4               C
          5           6           O
                                  P
              7                   E
              8
```

2 **Label the picture. Use the words from Activity 1.**

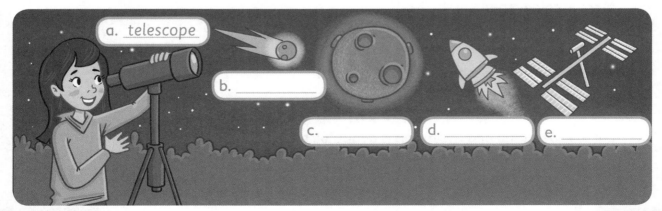

a. _telescope_

b. _____

c. _____

d. _____

e. _____

Lesson 2 Grammar

1 Unscramble the words to write sentences.

1 is / than / more / fun / walking to school / A spacewalk /.

   A spacewalk is more fun than walking to school.

2 as good as / . / Space food / isn't / home food

   _____

3 more / than / . / Earth / other planets / beautiful / is

   _____

4 the sun / as hot as / The moon / isn't / .

   _____

5 bigger / The space station / . / than / our school / is

   _____

2 Rewrite the sentences so that the meaning is the same. Use (not) as ... as and the adjective in brackets.

1 Mars is smaller than Earth. (big)

   Mars isn't as big as Earth.

2 A plane is slower than a spaceship. (fast)

   A plane _____

3 A spacewalk is more interesting than walking to school. (interesting)

   Walking to school _____

4 Mars is colder than Earth. (hot)

   Mars _____

5 The sun is brighter than the moon. (bright)

   The moon _____

6 Earth is beautiful and the moon is beautiful, too. (beautiful)

   Earth _____

1 Read. Then match the questions to the answers.

Ask an astronaut!

Send us your questions and we'll email them to Rick at the space station.

a **Ken**: Can you tell us about your daily routine? ☐

b **Amina**: What do you do in your free time? ☐

c **Finn**: How do you stay healthy? 1

d **Dev**: What clothes do you wear at the space station? ☐

To: Year5@ParkviewSchool.ac.uk

From: Rick@spacestation.com

Subject: My answers to your questions   SEND

Hello, everyone,

Thanks for all your questions! Here are my answers.

1 First of all, about exercise. Exercise is as important for us here as it is for you on Earth. We don't move around as much in the spaceship as we do on Earth, so it's harder to stay healthy. We have a running machine and I use that every day.

2 Everyone thinks we wear space suits every day. But it's not true! In the space station, we wear jeans and T-shirts. We wear the same clothes for a few days because we can't wash clothes in space! We only wear a space suit when we go on a spacewalk.

3 Every day, the space station plays music to wake us up in the morning! Then we get dressed. That's not as easy for us as it is for you! It takes longer to put our clothes on in space because they fly around the spaceship!

4 Some of us read, watch DVDs, or play musical instruments. I often just look out of the window. I look down at our beautiful planet and think of you all down there.

2 Complete.

1 It's harder to stay healthy on the space station because ___astronauts don't move___ ___around as much in the spaceship as they do on Earth.___

2 To stay healthy, Rick uses _____

3 Most of the time, astronauts wear _____

4 Astronauts don't change their clothes every day because they _____

5 To help them wake up, the space station _____

Lesson 4 Writing

1 Look at the Writing Tip. Write the best words to start and finish an email to:

1 … your aunt _____

2 … Mrs. Millar, your teacher _____

3 … your best friend _____

4 … your mom _____

> **Writing Tip!**
>
> • When we write an informal email, we use
> *Hi / Hello [name]*. To a very good friend of the
> same age, we can also use *Hey, [name]!*
>
> *Hi, Dad, / Hello, everyone at home, / Hey, Tomas!*
>
> • When we write a formal email, we use *Dear [name],*
>
> *Dear Mr. Bright,*
>
> • When we finish an informal email, we use *Love from
> [name], / Wish you were here, [name]*
>
> *Love from Dad, / Wish you were here, Jason*
>
> • When we finish a formal email, we use *Best wishes, [name]*
>
> *Best wishes, Mr. Bright*

2 Write your informal email. Use the information in Activity 2 on page 71 of your Student Book and the information above. Start and finish your email in the correct way.

To:

From:

Subject: SEND

Student Book page 71

1 Circle the six words. Then complete.

e	y	a	e	m	r	f	y
n	b	h	u	w	t	r	t
o	r	w	i	d	e	w	u
r	i	y	i	g	h	n	h
m	g	l	i	g	h	t	d
o	h	e	a	v	y	h	r
u	t	n	e	a	r	n	r
s	f	a	r	o	h	a	h

1 The Amazon is a very ____wide____ river. It takes a boat a long time to go across from one side to the other side.

2 I live _____ from school. I have to take a bus and a train to get to school every day. It's a long journey.

3 There's a park _____ my house. It's only five minutes away.

4 An elephant has two _____ teeth, called tusks. They're very long and heavy.

5 I can pick up my little kitten easily. He's very _____.

6 How _____ is a whale? About 50,000 kilograms!

7 The moon is very _____ tonight. It's shining into my window like a light.

2 Look at the circled words in Activity 1. Write.

1 Write two pairs of opposites.

a _____, _____

b _____, _____

2 Write a word that means very big. _____

Lesson 6 Grammar

1 Complete the questions. Use *long*, *wide*, *far*, *heavy*, and *tall*. Then match the questions to the answers.

1 How _____*far*_____ does an albatross bird fly every year?
2 How _____ is the largest polar bear?
3 How _____ is a python snake?
4 How _____ is the River Nile?
5 How _____ is a giraffe?

a 1,000 kilograms
b 2.8 kilometers
c 5–6 meters
d 15,000 kilometers
e More than 7 meters

2 Read the facts. Then write quiz questions. Use *far*, *heavy*, *hot*, *long*, and *wide*.

1 A hippo is about 1,500 kilograms.

   How heavy is a hippo?

2 Lake Victoria is 250 kilometers wide.

_____

3 It's about 384,400 kilometers from Earth to the moon.

_____

4 The Amazon River is 6,400 kilometers long.

_____

5 The sun is extremely hot. It's millions of degrees Fahrenheit!

_____

3 Write three more quiz questions for a friend. Use the words below.

(far   near   small)

1 _____
2 _____
3 _____

Student Book page 73

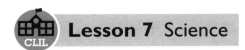

1 Circle the correct answers.

Eclipses

When the sun, the moon, and Earth are all in a line, it's called [1] **a shadow** / (**an eclipse**). An eclipse of the sun is called a solar eclipse, and an eclipse of the moon is a lunar eclipse. During a solar eclipse, the moon can hide [2] **the sun** / **Earth** for a few minutes. When the sun is behind the moon, there is a [3] **line** / **shadow** on Earth. When there's a total solar eclipse, you [4] **can see a shadow on the moon** / **can't see any light at all**. During a [5] **solar** / **lunar** eclipse, the moon looks red.

2 Read the texts on page 74 of your Student Book and in Activity 1 above. Then circle *True* or *False*.

1	Earth is as big as the sun.	True / (False)
2	Earth isn't as big as the moon.	True / False
3	Earth moves around the sun in 29.5 days.	True / False
4	There are two different kinds of eclipse.	True / False
5	The sun is further from Earth than the moon.	True / False
6	A solar eclipse is very bright.	True / False
7	During a lunar eclipse, there's a shadow over Earth.	True / False
8	There are up to 11 eclipses a year.	True / False

3 Answer the question.

What kind of eclipse is safe to look at? _____

Lesson 8 Word Study | Long and Short -oo-

1 Match the pictures to the words.

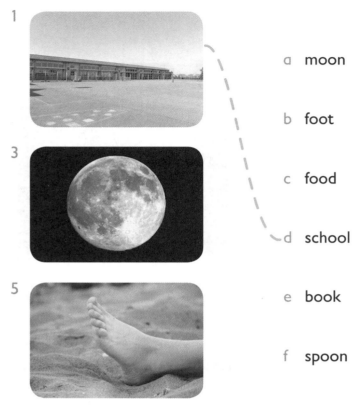

a moon

b foot

c food

d school

e book

f spoon

2 Look and complete. Use the words below.

cook   moo   good   room   food

1 He can ____cook____.

2 A cow can _____.

3 This is my _____.

1 Match the sentences (1–10) to the words (a–j).

1 You can see it at night. It's round, and it looks yellow or white. __e__

2 There are many in space. Ours is called Earth. _____

3 It's the place where astronauts work in space. _____

4 Astronauts travel into space in this. _____

5 _____ is the opposite of *near*.

6 _____ is the opposite of *light*.

7 _____ is the opposite of *very small*.

8 _____ is the opposite of *dark*.

9 We send _____ into space to collect information for us to use on Earth.

10 Our _____ consists of eight planets and their moons going around the sun.

a bright

b enormous

c far

d heavy

e the moon

f planets

g satellites

h solar system

i spaceship

j space station

2 Track it! Rate your progress in Unit 6.

I can name words about space. ☆☆☆☆☆

I can compare two things using *(not) as … as*. ☆☆☆☆☆

I can read and understand an informal email. ☆☆☆☆☆

I can write an informal email. ☆☆☆☆☆

I can name descriptive words. ☆☆☆☆☆

I can ask how long/far/big something is. ☆☆☆☆☆

I can read and understand a text about eclipses. ☆☆☆☆☆

I can explain the difference between solar and lunar eclipses. ☆☆☆☆☆

I can read and say words with long and short *-oo-*. ☆☆☆☆☆

Share the World 3 | An African Folktale

1 **Read the folktale on page 78 of your Student Book. Circle the best title for the folktale.**

a Why the Sea Is Full of Fish

b Why the Sun and the Moon Live in the Sky

c Why the Sea Is so Big

2 **Unscramble the words and write the answers.**

1 The top of a house   orfo   _roof_

2 Very big   omrosenu   _____

3 You say this when people come to visit you.   lwcmoee   _____

4 How big something is from one side to the other side.   ewid   _____

5 The planet where Water still lives.   trhEa   _____

3 **Circle the correct answers.**

1 Water didn't visit Sun's house very often because …

   a Sun's house was bigger than Water's house.

   b Sun's house was too small.

2 Moon lived in the same house as …

   a Sun.   b Water.

3 The first time Water visited Sun's new house, …

   a she had a lot of friends with her.

   b she was alone.

4 Sun and Moon climbed up to the roof because …

   a they didn't like Water's friends.

   b the house was full of fish, other animals, and water.

5 When the water was as high as the roof, …

   a Water and her friends went home.

   b Sun and Moon went far up into space.

4 Think. Answer the questions.

1 Do you think Water was a good friend? Why / Why not?

_____

_____

2 Do you think Sun and Moon are happy living in the solar system? Why? / Why not?

_____

_____

5 Read, think, and draw.

One night, Star and her friends came to visit Sun and Moon in their house in the solar system. What happened? Was their house big enough for the stars? Did they like it there?

_____

6 Think. What is a good friend? Write.

A good friend always …

_____

_____

A good friend never …

_____

_____

Lesson 1 Vocabulary

1 Match the parts of the words.

1	3D		a	worker
2	flying		b	car
3	electric		c	pack
4	VR		d	board
5	robot		e	printer
6	jet		f	headset
7	hover		g	bike

2 Look and write.

1 _____drone_____

2 _____

3 _____

4 _____

5 _____

6 _____

3 Which two items are missing from Activity 2? Write and draw.

1 _____

2 _____

1 **Write *will* (✔) or *won't* (✗).**

1 Everyone / have a drone in the future ✔

   Everyone will have a drone in the future.

2 Taylor / ride a hoverboard to school in the future ✔

   _____

3 Sarah go to school / on an electric bike ✗

   _____

4 In the future, people / work ✗

   _____

5 Robot workers / do all the work ✔

   _____

2 **Look and circle *True* or *False*.**

1 We'll fly to school with jetpacks.	True / (False)
2 I want a drone! It will be fun!	True / False
3 In school, we'll use 3D printers to make things.	True / False
4 My dad won't ride an electric bike. He'll buy a flying car!	True / False
5 Robot workers will be doctors.	True / False

Lesson 3 Reading

1 Read. Then circle the best name for the robot worker.

1 Harry, the Home Helper   2 Robbie, the Homework Robot   3 Katie, the Kitchen Robot

HOME ROBOT

| Home | About Us | Products | Contact Us |

What is it?

Do you need help with cooking, cleaning, gardening, and getting ready for school? Buy a robot worker! You won't have to do any of these things again!

What will it do?

It will take out the trash, clean the floor, and walk the dog. It is also a 3D printer. It will print things you need, for example, bowls, plates, and new toys!

The robot worker will even play a game with you. It's very good at chess. It will help you study for a test. There's only one thing you should know. It won't do your homework for you! 😊

How to use it

Just press ON and tell it what you want. There is only one problem with the robot worker. It won't know when to stop. So ... say *Stop*!

Go to your nearest computer store today and buy the new robot worker. You'll love it!

2 Read again. Then write.

1 Write three things the robot worker will do.

_____

_____

_____

2 Write one thing the robot worker won't do.

_____

3 Write one instruction.

_____

4 Write one warning.

_____

5 Write where you can buy the robot worker. _____

1 Look at the Writing Tip. Add the missing apostrophes in these sentences.

1 I'm not going to make my bed. Its the robots job!

2 My robot workers name is Mario.

3 It tidies my room, but it doesnt tidy my parents room.

> **Writing Tip!** Use an apostrophe:
> - for contractions. *I'll ride a hoverboard one day. I won't fly with a jetpack.*
> - to show possession. *This is my dad's flying car. These are my friends' electric bikes.*

2 Write your user guide. Then draw. Use the information in Activity 2 on page 85 of your Student Book. Remember to add apostrophes.

Machine's name: _____

What it does: _____

_____

_____

_____

Instructions: _____

_____

_____

_____

Warnings: _____

_____

Where to buy: _____

_____

Lesson 5 Vocabulary

1 Circle the words. Then write.

(greenbuildings)jeskyscrapertenergypasmarthomecautomatickdriverlesscarsdrinventionsontravele

1 These places have trees and plants all over them, so they are healthy. _green buildings_

2 This kind of machine doesn't need people to turn it on and off. _____

3 Flying cars, hoverboards, and electric bikes are all examples of _____ that will help us to _____ a lot faster.

4 This kind of house or apartment uses a lot of technology to make things easy.

_____ _____

5 This is a very tall building where people live or work. _____

6 In the future, people won't need to drive, because there will be these.

_____ _____

7 Plants get this from the sun. _____

2 Use the extra letters in the wordsnake to write two more inventions that will help people in the future.

1 _____

2 _____

1 Write yes/no questions about the future.

1 we / have cars

  Will we have cars?

2 robots / be our teachers

  _____

3 I / live in a smart home

  _____

4 my sister / travel to school in a jetpack

  _____

5 cars / be slower than they are now

  _____

6 you / have to do your own shopping

  _____

2 Answer the questions in Activity 1. Use _will_ or _won't_.

1 Yes, we _____will_____ . But we _____won't_____ drive them. They'_ll_____ be driverless cars!

2 No, they _____ . Our teachers _____ be people.

3 Yes, you _____ . Everything in your home _____ be automatic!

4 Yes, she _____ . Everyone _____ use jetpacks!

5 No, they _____ . They _____ be a lot faster.

6 No, you _____ . Your refrigerator _____ do your shopping!

3 Write two more questions about the future.

  _____

  _____

Lesson 7 Science CLIL

1 Complete. Use the words below.

> companies   ~~delivery~~   driverless
> modern   safely   wheels   wings

James: In the future, we will order food and other items online. How will these things arrive at our homes?

Laura: 1 _Delivery_ drones will bring them.

James: People say that cars won't have drivers in the future. I'm worried that these 2 _____ cars will be dangerous. Will people drive 3 _____ on the roads?

Laura: Yes, they will! Driverless cars won't be dangerous, because 4 _____ technology will make them very safe. We'll also have flying cars!

James: What are they?

Laura: They're cars that will use 5 _____ to fly! They will also have four 6 _____ so that they can drive on roads, too.

James: Will it be a long time before we see these amazing new inventions?

Laura: No, it won't. Some 7 _____ are already making them.

James: Wow! Transportation will definitely be very different in the future!

2 Circle the correct answers.

1 In the future, cars won't need **(drivers)** / **wheels**.

2 Driverless cars will have **wings** / **video cameras** to see the lines on the road.

3 Many people say machines will be good drivers because they get **more** / **less** tired than people.

4 In the future, when you drive a car, you **will** / **won't** also be able to read a book.

5 There **will** / **won't** be too many cars on the roads in the future, because a lot of cars will **deliver** / **fly**.

Student Book pages 88-

1 Complete. Use the words below.

| sauce | walks | ball | ~~straw~~ | salt | talk |

1

Please can I have a
___straw___ for my drink?

2

I won't have any
_____, thanks.

3

They like to _____
a lot.

4

This _____ is
delicious, Dad!

5

He _____ to
work every day.

6

I'll play with the
_____ later!

2 Unscramble the words.

1

Look! I can (wrad) ___draw___
a (ndsoriau) _____!

2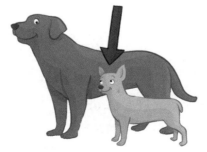

My friend's dog is very
(mslal) _____.

3

An eagle's (aclws)
_____ are
very strong.

Progress Tracker

1 Match the sentences (1–10) to the words (a–j).

1 This kind of car doesn't need a driver. _a_

2 You use it to play computer games. _____

3 You stand on it, and it moves along the ground. _____

4 It can fly into very small spaces and deliver things. _____

5 It can clean your house. _____

6 People will wear these to fly! _____

7 It's a very tall building. _____

8 This kind of house has a lot of technology and automatic inventions. _____

9 You get this from the sun. ___

10 People build this kind of place with a lot of plants and trees. _____

a driverless

b drone

c energy

d green building

e hoverboard

f jetpack

g robot worker

h skyscraper

i smart home

j VR headset

2 Track it! Rate your progress in Unit 7.

I can name high-tech inventions. ☆☆☆☆☆

I can talk about the future using *will* and *won't*. ☆☆☆☆☆

I can read and understand a user guide. ☆☆☆☆☆

I can write a user guide. ☆☆☆☆☆

I can describe life in the future. ☆☆☆☆☆

I can ask yes/no questions about the future. ☆☆☆☆☆

I can read and understand a text about future transportation. ☆☆☆☆☆

I can talk about future transportation. ☆☆☆☆☆

I can read and say words with *-au-*, *-aw-*, *-all*, *-alk*, and *-alt*. ☆☆☆☆☆

Lesson 1 Vocabulary

1 Look at the pictures and complete the crossword.

Down

1

2

4

Across

3

5

6

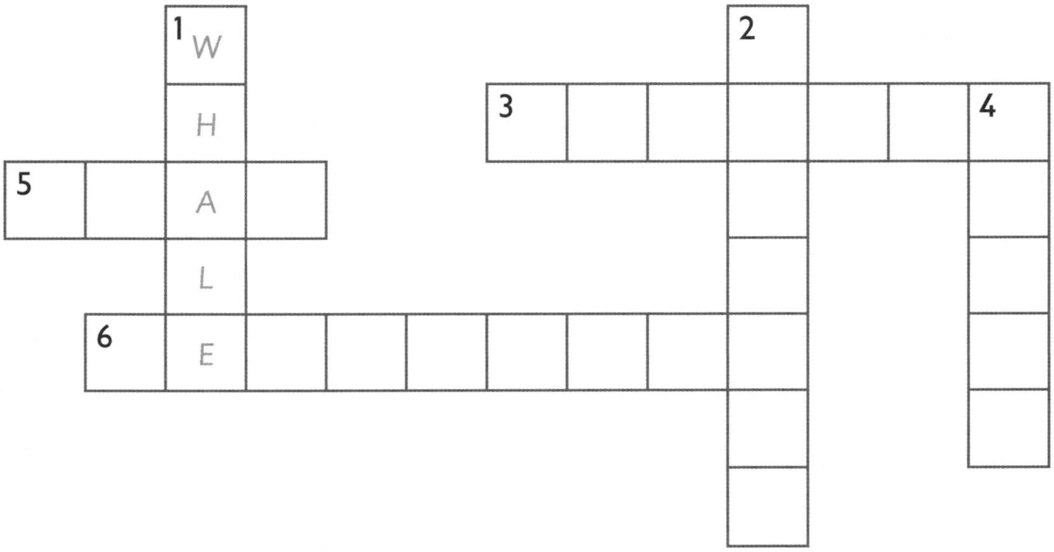

2 Complete the words.

a

The [1] o ___ ___ ___ n

b

The [2] c ___ r ___ l r ___ ___ f

Lesson 2 Grammar

1 Complete. Use *will* and the verbs in brackets.

1 What _____*will*_____ _____*happen*_____ (happen) to the ice in the Arctic? It will melt.

2 What _____(happen) to the ocean? It will become warmer.

3 What _____ the crabs and small fish _____(do)? They'll leave the coral reef.

4 What animals _____ (eat) the small fish? Sharks will eat them.

5 What _____ (happen) to the coral reefs? They won't grow.

2 Make questions about the future. Then complete the answers.

1 People throw trash into the oceans. What / happen / to the fish? They / die.

   What will happen to the fish? They'll die.

2 People drive cars in cities. What / happen / to the air? It / be / dirtier.

   _____

3 In the future, there won't be many fish to eat. What / people / eat / in the future? They / eat / plants.

   _____

4 People cut down trees. What / happen / to the forest animals? They / not have / homes.

   _____

5 What / people / do / when the beaches are full of trash? They / clean / them.

   _____

Student Book page 93

1 Read the interview. Then match the questions to the answers.

My interview with a **Marine Biologist** *By Evan*

Today I'm talking to Francesca. She has a very interesting life!

1 Can you tell us about your job? _d_
2 Which is your favorite marine animal? _____
3 Did you grow up by the sea? _____
4 What will happen to marine life in the future? _____
5 Is there anything we can do to help? _____

a Everyone can try to use less plastic. That way, most of our plastic trash won't end up in the ocean.

b The sea is getting warmer, and many fish can't live in warm water. But trash in the ocean is the biggest problem. One day, there will be more plastic in the ocean than fish! Many marine animals will die because of this.

c I love all marine animals, but dolphins are my favorite! They are the friendliest and they're very smart.

d Well, I research marine animals in the oceans around New Zealand. We study whales and dolphins. I spend one day a week in a laboratory, and the rest of the week, I'm in the sea!

e Yes, when I was a child, we lived by the ocean. I spent all my free time in the sea and on the beach. I loved looking at jellyfish and crabs! But the planet is changing now, and life in the oceans is changing, too.

2 Answer the questions.

1 How did Francesca become interested in the ocean?

She lived by the ocean when she was a child.

2 What is a typical week like for Francesca?

_____

3 Why does she like dolphins so much?

_____

4 Why is warmer water in our oceans dangerous for fish?

_____

5 What is the biggest problem for marine life?

_____

Lesson 4 Writing

1 Look at the Writing Tip. Rewrite the sentences.

1 are / dolphins and whales, / Many / for example, / animals, / smart / very.

_____

2 studies / Francesca / like / animals / turtles and crabs.

_____

3 biology and science / Subjects / useful / are / for future marine biologists / such as.

_____

> **Writing Tip!** Use _like_, _such as_, and _for example_ to give examples.
> I work with marine animals, **like** whales and dolphins.
> Many small animals **such as** crabs and turtles live in coral reefs.
> A lot of trash, **for example**, plastic, goes into the ocean.

2 Write your interview dialogue. Use the answers in Activity 2 on page 95 of your Student Book. Use _like_, _such as_, and _for example_ when you give examples.

My interview with _____ _By_ _____

_____

_____

_____

_____

_____

_____

_____

_____

Student Book page 95

1 Complete. Use the words below.

electricity   environment   lights   recycling bins
reuse   s~~av~~e   turn off   waste

1 ___Save___ the 2 _____ !

REDUCE

Don't 3 _____ 4 _____ .
Always 5 _____ _____ the TV, radio, and
any computers in a room when you are not using them.
Do the same for any 6 _____ !

REUSE

Don't use a new plastic bag every day to carry your lunch in.
It's better to 7 _____ a bag or box.

RECYCLE

Don't throw trash away.
Look for 8 _____ _____ that can
reuse glass, paper, card, and plastic.

2 Look at Activity 1. Find the words.

1 Write two opposites.

_____ , _____

2 Write two words that mean *to use again*.

_____ , _____

Lesson 6 Grammar

1 Write six different sentences. Use a word or phrase from each column.

When we

don't recycle
don't take
don't turn off
recycle
take
turn off

bottles, bags, and clothes,
computers,
lights,
long baths,
our phones,
short showers,

we reduce
we save
we waste
we make more

electricity.
trash.
water.

1   *When we don't take long baths, we save water.*

2   _____

3   _____

4   _____

5   _____

6   _____

2 Complete with your own ideas.

1   When we ride our bikes, we

_____

2   When we don't do our homework, we

_____

3   When we reuse a bag or box,

_____

4   When we eat a lot of fruits and vegetables,
    we _____

5   When we take long showers, we _____

6   When we don't sleep very much, we _____

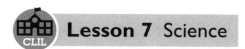

1 Match the parts of the sentences.

Wind Energy

1 Climate change is when Earth   d   a   collect energy from the sun and make electricity.

2 Renewable energy   ☐   b   makes electricity.

3 Solar panels   ☐   c   is land with the sea on all sides.

4 Solar energy   ☐   d   becomes warmer and the weather changes.

5 A wind turbine   ☐   e   comes from the sun, the wind, or water.

6 An island   ☐   f   comes from the sun.

2 Read the text on page 98 of your Student Book again. Circle the correct answers.

1 Climate change is happening because we are using …

   (a) too much energy.   b renewable energy.

2 When we reduce trash, we …

   a waste energy.   b help Earth.

3 Renewable energy …

   a causes pollution.   b doesn't cause pollution.

4 Places with a lot of sun are good for …

   a solar energy.   b wave energy.

5 You can only have wind farms …

   a on islands.   b in places where there is a lot of wind.

Solar Energy

Lesson 8 Word Study -air, -are, -ear

1 Match the pictures to the words.

1
2

a chair

b pear

3
4

c bear

d share

5
6

e hair

f square

2 Look and complete. Use the words below.

| stairs | scare | wear |

1
2
3

She likes to _____ a big hat!

The _____ are very wide.

This spider doesn't _____ me!

1 Match the sentences (1–10) to the words (a–j).

1 It's the biggest, heaviest sea animal. _j_

2 It lives in the coral reef. It has a hard shell. _____

3 It has eight "legs." _____

4 We can save this in many ways. _____

5 These are special containers for plastic, paper, and glass. _____

6 This means to use something again and again. _____

7 You waste electricity when you don't do this. _____

8 It's a gray, friendly sea animal. _____

9 It's the sea. _____

10 It's a beautiful, colorful part of the ocean where many small fish live. _____

a recycling bins

b coral reef

c crab

d dolphin

e environment

f ocean

g octopus

h reuse

i turn off lights

j whale

2 Track it! **Rate your progress in Unit 8.**

I can name ocean words.

I can ask questions about the future.

I can read and understand an interview.

I can write a short interview dialogue.

I can name words and phrases about saving the planet.

I can use *when* to talk about the future.

I can read and understand a text about renewable energy.

I can give a presentation about renewable energy.

I can read and say words with *-air*, *-are*, and *-ear*.

1 Why did the writer write the article? Circle the correct answer.

a To encourage tourists to visit Australia.

b To help us to learn about the Great Barrier Reef.

c To tell us about famous places to visit in Australia.

2 Which of the following information is <u>not</u> in the article? Check (✔).

1 Why dugongs are endangered ☐

2 What dugongs look like ☐

3 Why many turtles are dying ☐

4 How scientists are helping to save the Great Barrier Reef ☐

5 How big the Great Barrier Reef is ☐

6 The names of the seven natural wonders of the world ☐

3 Match the numbers to the information.

1 25 million

2 2,300

3 200

4 70

5 2

a How many babies a mother dugong will have in 10 years

b The number of species of birds that live in the Great Barrier Reef

c How many years a dugong can live

d How old the Great Barrier Reef is

e How long the Great Barrier Reef is, in kilometers

4 Think. Answer the questions.

1 Would you like to visit the Great Barrier Reef? Why / Why not?

....

....

2 How do you think we can help endangered animals in our everyday lives?

....

....

....

5 Why is it important to take care of Earth and our environment?

....

....

....

6 Think and draw.

Are there any endangered animals in your country? Draw an endangered animal that you know about. Then label your drawing.

Word Work Unit 1

1 Complete. Use the words below.

a campfire	a shelter	~~hiking~~	canoeing	mountain biking	a tent
	horseback riding		a zipline		

1 You go ... _____hiking_____ _____ _____ _____

2 You ride on ... _____

3 You cook on ... _____

4 You sleep in ... _____   You build ... _____

2 Write the phrases. Use the words below and other words you need.

go ×3   play ×3   jump on   ~~make~~

 1 _____make jewelry_____

 2 _____

 3 _____

 4 _____

 5 _____

 6 _____

 7 _____

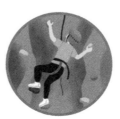 8 _____

1 Complete. Then sort and write.

1

sunbathe

2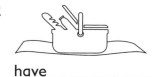

have _____

3

build _____

4

go _____

5

build _____

6

have _____

7

eat _____

8

learn to _____

a Three beach activities: _____ _____ _____

b Two activities for snow: _____ _____

c Two activities with food: _____ _____

d You do this indoors or outdoors, with food or without food: _____

2 Complete. Then match the pictures to the words.

1

2

a play the d _____ m _____

b d____ g_____ n_____ t_____ ____ s

3

4

c a_____ i____ a p__ a____

d s_____ i____ a b___ n____

1 Complete. Then match the pictures to the words.

buy ×2   play   read   study for   take out   ~~walk~~   watch

a _____walk_____ the dog [5]   b _____ the news on TV [ ]

c _____ _____ a test [ ]   d _____ chess [ ]

e _____ groceries [ ]   f _____ the trash [ ]

g _____ the newspaper [ ]   h _____ a present [ ]

2 Complete. Use the words below.

online   the radio   ~~magazines~~   an app   a screen   a blog post

1 You read …	2 You download …	3 You go …	4 You look at …	5 You listen to …
magazines				

1 Complete. Use the words below.

| sick   cold   good   ~~headache~~   stomach ache   sore throat   toothache   fever |

1 have a __headache__

2 have a _____ _____

3 have a _____

4 have a _____

5 feel _____

6 have a _____ _____

7 have a _____

8 feel _____

2 Unscramble the words.

1 A headache and a sore throat are (tomsymsp) __symptoms__ of a cold.

2 Your head feels very hot. I think you have a (paertemtuer) _____.

3 Cover your mouth with a tissue when you (uoghc) _____.

4 I'll go to the (maphcyra) _____ to buy you something to make you feel better.

5 Do you feel sick? You should (iel) _____ down for a while.

6 I feel terrible! I have the (luf) _____.

7 Take two teaspoons of this (dicmeine) _____. It will help your sore throat.

Word Work Unit 5

1 Look and write.

1

olives

2

_____

3

_____

4

_____

5

_____

6

_____

7

_____

8

_____

9

_____

2 Complete. Then match the pictures to the words.

1 p l a t e   b

2 b _____ _____ l

3 g _____ _____ s _____

4 k _____ _____ _____ e

5 c _____ _____

6 t _____ _____ s _____ _____ _____ n

7 f _____ _____ k

8 t _____ _____ _____ _____
   s _____ _____ _____ n

1 Look and write.

1

telescope

2

3

4

5

6
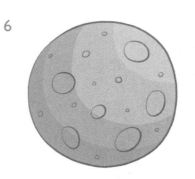

2 Look and write two adjectives for each picture. Use the words below.

bright   enormous   far   heavy   ~~near~~   wide

①

near

②

③

Word Work Unit 7

1 Complete. Then match the pictures to the words.

a r _____ _____ t w _____ _____ k _____ _____ ☐

b e _____ _____ c _____ _____ _____ c b _____ _____ e ☐

c d _____ _____ n _____ ☐

d f _____ _____ i _____ _____ c _____ _____ ☐

e j _e_ _t_ p _a_ _c_ k [1]

f _____ D p _____ _____ _____ t _____ _____ ☐

1  2  3

4  5  6

2 Unscramble the words.

1 I can't drive. But I can drive a (srelsrived) __driverless__ car!

2 One day, we'll all (velrat) _____ to school on hoverboards.

3 In a (tarsm oehm) _____ _____, everything is (ticamtauo) _____.

4 I live in a (regen bidgunli) _____ _____. It's full of plants and trees.

5 That (pycersksra) _____ is about 80 meters tall!

6 The sun gives us a lot of (greeny) _____.

7 A drone is a modern (oniventni) _____.

Student Book pages 82 and 86

1 Look and write.

1

shark

2

3

4

5
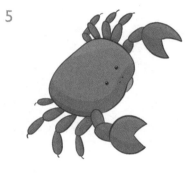

6

2 Complete. Use the words below.

> ~~turn off lights~~   leave the TV on   recycle old clothes   leave the computer on
> not turning off water when we brush our teeth   having long showers

1 Ways We Can Save the Environment	2 Ways We Waste Electricity	3 Ways We Waste Water
turn off lights		

Macmillan Education Limited
4 Crinan Street
London N1 9XW

Companies and representatives throughout the world

Share It! Level 5 Workbook ISBN 978-1-380-02314-8

Share It! Level 5 Workbook and Digital Workbook
ISBN 978-1-380-06943-6

Text, design and illustration © Macmillan Education Limited 2020
Written by Cheryl Pelteret

Word Study lessons written by Wiley Blevins

The author has asserted their right to be identified as the author of this work in accordance with the Copyright, Designs and Patents Act 1988.

Share It! is a registered trademark published by Macmillan Education Limited

First published 2020

Original design by Pronk Media, Inc.
Page make-up by SPi Global
Illustrated by Giuliano Aloisi (Advocate Art) pp. 26– 27; Alla Badsar (Advocate Art) pp. 18– 19, 46; Juan Calle (Advocate Art) p. 66; Dan Crisp (The Bright Agency) pp. 15, 23, 24, 35, 44, 89, 91; Tom Heard (The Bright Agency) pp. 54– 55, 64, 75, 84, 92– 93, 95; Emi Ordás & Wedoo Studio pp. 4, 9, 11, 16, 18, 20, 25, 29, 31, 36, 38, 40, 45, 49, 51, 56, 58, 60, 65, 69, 71, 76, 78, 80, 82, 85; Noopur Thakur (Advocate Art) pp. 12, 88; Dave Williams (The Bright Agency) pp. 5, 6 – 7, 9, 10, 13, 21, 22, 29, 30, 33, 37, 38, 41, 42, 48, 49, 50, 52– 53, 56, 57, 61, 62, 69, 70, 79, 81, 94.
Cover illustration by Emi Ordás
Cover photographs by Getty Images/E+/SDI Productions, Getty Images/iStock/FatCamera
Picture research by Sarah Wells

The authors and publishers would like to thank the following for permission to reproduce their photographs:

123RF/lightfieldstudios p. 8(8);

Alamy Stock Photo/Classic Image p. 14, Alamy Stock Photo/Cultura RM p. 8(1);

Comstock p. 75(2);

Getty Images p. 24(4), Getty Images/500px/gopro8o8hi p. 77(a), Getty Images/Blend Images/JGI/Jamie Grill p. 15(2), Getty Images/Blend Images/Jose Luis Pelaez Inc pp. 28(a), 90(1), Getty Images/Blend Images/Klaus Tiedge p. 17(6), Getty Images/Brand X Pictures/Gallo Images p. 24(1), Getty Images/BrandX Pictures/Westend61/Gerald Nowak p. 15(1), Getty Images/Brian E. Kushner p. 64(3), Getty Images/Corbis/Fuse p. 35(6), Getty Images/Digital Vision Vectors/duncan1890 p. 34, Getty Images/E+/4kodiak p. 24(2), Getty Images/E+/clubfoto p. 64(1), Getty Images/E+/gaspr13 p. 8(7), Getty Images/E+/Imgorthand p. 17(2), Getty Images/E+/Juanmonino pp. 28(b), 90(2), Getty Images/E+/letty17 p. 84(1), Getty Images/E+/oversnap p. 63, Getty Images/E+/skodonnell p. 24(6), Getty Images/E+/Steve Debenport pp. 28(g), 90(7), Getty Images/EyeEm/Nirut Teerakarunkarn p. 75(5), Getty Images/EyeEm/Ramzi Rizk p. 64(6), Getty Images/EyeEm/Richard Casteel p. 83(1), Getty Images/EyeEm/Robert Alvarez p. 84(6), Getty Images/fStop/Halfdark pp. 28(d), 90(4), Getty Images/Hero Images pp. 8(3), 28(f), 90(6), Getty Images/Hoxton/Tom Merton p. 17(3), Getty Images/Image Source p. 17(1), Getty Images/iStock/Ales-A p. 55(4), Getty Images/iStock/baibaz p. 75(1), Getty Images/iStock/bajinda p. 35(3), Getty Images/iStock/bonetta p. 15(6), Getty Images/iStock/Chalabala p. 15(4), Getty Images/iStock/Chesky_W p. 73, Getty Images/iStock/dimdimich p. 55(1), Getty Images/iStock/dreamnikon p. 68(5), Getty Images/iStock/fallbrook p. 68(6), Getty Images/iStock/Garsya p. 24(3), Getty Images/iStock/HughStonelan p. 55(5), Getty Images/iStock/Ismailciydem p. 44(1), Getty Images/iStock/jamesteohart p. 77(1), Getty Images/iStock/Jovanmandic p. 8(2), Getty Images/iStock/juliedeshaies p. 75(4), Getty Images/iStock/Magnascan p. 55(2), Getty Images/iStock/Marje p. 44(3), Getty Images/iStock/michaeljung p. 55(3), Getty Images/iStock/nigelb10 p. 35(1), Getty Images/iStock/Pakhnyushchyy p. 44(6), Getty Images/iStock/PhonlamaiPhoto p. 74, Getty Images/iStock/pinkomelet p. 15(5), Getty Images/iStock/quintanilla p. 35(4), Getty Images/iStock/rzymu p. 44(5), Getty Images/iStock/Smileus p. 83(2), Getty Images/iStock/specnaz-s p. 64(4), Getty Images/iStock/subjug p. 84(3), Getty Images/iStock/TheSP4N1SH p. 77(3), Getty Images/iStock/Tomwang112 p. 84(4), Getty Images/iStock/vlad61 p. 77(b), Getty Images/iStock/Vladimiroquai p. 24(5), Getty Images/iStock/xenicx p. 64(2), Getty Images/iStockphoto/Thinkstock Images p. 86, Getty Images/Moment/Dmitry Miroshnikov p. 77(4), Getty Images/Moment/john finney photography p. 35(5), Getty Images/Moment/Rodrigo Valença p. 77(5), Getty Images/Monkey Business Images p. 75(3), Getty Images/PhotoAlto Agency RF Collections/Odilon Dimier p. 17(5), Getty Images/PhotoObjects.net/Hemera Technologies p. 84(5), Getty Images/Radius Images pp. 28(c), 90(3), Getty Images/Steve Debenport p. 68(4), Getty Images/Steve Stone p. 8(5), Getty Images/Thinkstock/Ryan McVay p. 35(2), Getty Images/Westend61 p. 8(4), Getty Images/Westend61 p. 17(7), Getty Images/EyeEm/Eskay Lim pp. 28(h), 90(8);

Image Source/Steve Prezant p. 84(2);

Photodisc p. 44(4), Photodisc/Getty Images p. 59;

Macmillan Education Limited/ Paul Bricknell p. 75(6);

Stockbyte p. 55(6);

Shutterstock/Studio 1One p. 8(6), Shutterstock/Andrea Izzotti p. 77(5), Shutterstock/Arve Bettum p. 64(5), Shutterstock/bonvoyagecaptain p. 77(6), Shutterstock/Carboxylase p. 18-19, Shutterstock/DimaBerlin p. 43, Shutterstock/Dmitry Kalinovsky p. 68(1), Shutterstock/iurii p. 72, Shutterstock/JFs Pic S. Thielemann p. 68(2), Shutterstock/Kasefoto p. 32, Shutterstock/Konstantin Tronin pp. 28(e), 44(2), 90(5), Shutterstock/Monkey Business Images p. 15(3), Shutterstock/Neirfy p. 17(4), Shutterstock/Sergey Novikov p. 17(8), Shutterstock/Pascal Theune p. 68(3).

Printed and bound in Poland by CGS

2025 2024 2023 2022 2021

18 17 16 15 14 13 12 11 10 9